WE GO SEASONAL

WE GO SEASONAL

Robert Siek

SIBLING RIVALRY PRESS
LITTLE ROCK, ARKANSAS
DISTURB / ENRAPTURE

We Go Seasonal
Copyright © 2018 by Robert Siek.
Cover art by Blake Neubert as photographed by Christian Ledan Photography. Used by permission.
Author photo by Christian Ledan Photography.
Cover design by Seth Pennington.

All rights reserved. No part of this book may be reproduced or republished without written consent from the publisher, except by reviewers who may quote brief excerpts in connection with a review in a newspaper, magazine, or electronic publication; nor may any part of this book be reproduced, stored in a retrieval system, or transmitted in any form, or by any means be recorded without written consent of the publisher.

Sibling Rivalry Press, LLC
PO Box 26147
Little Rock, AR 72221
info@siblingrivalrypress.com
www.siblingrivalrypress.com

ISBN: 978-1-943977-51-2
Library of Congress Control No. 2018941802

This title is housed permanently in the Rare Books and Special Collections Vault of the Library of Congress.

First Sibling Rivalry Press Edition, September 2018

To my parents, Joan and Joseph Siek

CONTENTS

13 *Acknowledgments*

17 Cat Burglar

Part I: Out with the Old

21 Gay Life During Wartime
23 An Introvert Travels with Gifts
25 Dead by Dawn
26 1993
28 We Go Together
30 Sometimes Satanic
32 What's Your Damage?
35 Never Go Down and Cause Fires
36 Bang Bang Behind an Aquarium
38 Hand Wash
40 Strays
42 Black and White
43 Incredible Hulk
45 On Preferring Unscented
46 Spaced Out
47 Runners Love Ghosts
48 This Is Called Making It
50 Color Me Bored, 2014
52 Gay Vikings in Love

53	Downtown Reading on a Rainy Day
54	When Poets Attack
56	Satan Says Fuck the First Hot Piece of Ass You See on the Subway
57	Cold Life Over Young Chins

Part II: In with the New

61	We Go Seasonal
62	Slip'N Slide
63	Some Birds Are Smarter Than Others
64	I'm Not Mad at You; I'm Mad at the Dirt
65	Hell Mouth Ends in Green
66	Neverland Gets Crowded
68	Close Encounters
70	We Do Hospitals and Leave
71	Doomed Here
73	We Float Like Marshmallows
74	Fireworks Are Illegal in My Home State
75	I've Got My Eyes on You
77	How to Remain Active in July
79	Take Me to the River
80	No Place Like Home
82	It's a Rich Man's World
83	Marshland Merriment
85	Let Me Hear Your Body Talk
86	Living in the Ice Age

87	Then I Saw Another Beast Coming Up Out of the Earth
89	Cruisin' for a Bruisin'
91	Go, Indie, Go
92	Misty Watercolor Memories of the Way We Were
93	This Guest Room Must Be Haunted
95	I've Had the Time of My Life
97	Just Say No
98	Useful Man
100	Flooding Basements at Six Flags Guantanamo Park
102	Thelma and Louis (Spoiler Alert: We Don't Drive Off a Cliff)
104	Bounty
106	Born in the U.S.A.
108	Part Two
110	Letting the Days Go By

ACKNOWLEDGMENTS

I'd like to thank the editors of the following publications where some of the poems in this collection were previously published (sometimes as somewhat different versions):

The Nervous Breakdown: "Gay Life During Wartime"

Estrellas en el Fuego 2014 Anthology: "Bang Bang Behind an Aquarium"

The Gay and Lesbian Review Worldwide: "Gay Vikings in Love"

Assaracus: "We Go Seasonal"

Vaczine: "Hand Wash"

Brooklyn Poets "Poet of the Week" feature: "Close Encounters"

visceral brooklyn: "Flooding Basements at Six Flags Guantanamo Park," "Thelma and Louis (Spoiler Alert: We Don't Drive Off a Cliff)," and "Part Two"

NANCY: "Then I Saw Another Beast Coming Up Out of the Earth"

Brooklyn Poets Anthology: "We Do Hospitals and Leave"

Bushwick Daily: "Incredible Hulk"

Court Green: "Born in the U.S.A.," "This Guest Room Must Be Haunted," and "What's Your Damage?"

Columbia Poetry Review: "I'm Not Mad at You; I'm Mad at the Dirt" and "Bounty"

Impossible Archetype: "Cruisin' for a Bruisin'"

Thank you to the following people for past positive feedback and for doing or saying something at some point that pushed me to continue writing my ridiculous poems: Jeffery Berg, Charlie Bondhus, Michael Carasone, Dennis Cooper, Lynn Crosbie (the goddess, beloved friend, and fellow worshipper of the Love Rats), Wayne Koestenbaum, Timothy Liu, Stephen Mills, David Trinidad (personal poetry idol, fellow pop enthusiast, and mentor-turned-friend), and Emanual Xavier. Tremendous thank you to my publishers and editors Bryan Borland and Seth Pennington; they continue to believe in me and my work, and it's not even possible for me to communicate the amount of appreciation I have for them and Sibling Rivalry Press.

I'd also like to thank my family and friends for their constant support, despite the fact that most of them are not regular poetry readers. Finally I'd like to thank my boyfriend, Ryan Collier, for always being honest with me when asked to say what he thought of a new poem and for always being by my side.

I remember trying to figure things out—(life)—trying to get it all down to something basic—and ending up with nothing. Except a dizzy head.

– Joe Brainard, *I Remember*

CAT BURGLAR

A big o' bag of diamonds,
Swarovski crystals
dumped in a waterfall,
melting glacier surfed on,
noon and sunburned,
poets full of it,
everything
on the menu,
I'll Cracker Barrel you
to death, bury you in tchotchkes,
every state. Are you ready?
Are you ready? Are you ready?

PART I
OUT WITH THE OLD

GAY LIFE DURING WARTIME

I want Heidi Klum to say, "Kill for me designers,"
patting Tim Gunn's back while brandishing a sword.
It can start a true social war, provoke liberal men
of unknown sexual preference, feminine homosexuals
who get bitchy over fashion, older women
in the business, years choosing to stay gray,
other free-spirited gals, supporters of gay rights,
one of whom is a lesbian, she said so the first episode.
It will be a Stonewall riot starting at Parsons,
thirtysomething street, midtown Manhattan,
where they'll be joined by fabric-store workers;
editorial assistants from *Elle, Vogue,* and *W;*
multiple casting agents from popular modeling agencies;
publicists; hard hats; stock brokers; police officers.
Members of the military land helicopters in Times Square,
pack them full, then fly past state lines
to drop bombs on Chick-fil-As, make out
on green lawns, roll like teenagers' first times
on red-and-white checkered tablecloths,
tackle family-first supporters protesting at funerals,
signs above their heads that read, "Jesus Hates Fags"
or "Homos Go to Hell," but no slit throats or bullets
through chests, instead we run through Walmarts,
pop shots off handguns toward ceilings,
get shoppers' attention, tickle strangers
while teammates hold arms, pull down pants

and expose genitals to spit on,
but nothing sexual. No bloodshed
behind Heidi's cry for battle,
just crew cuts on high-styled Christian housewives
eating fried chicken from paper bags, makeup on
their husbands tied to trees with hosiery, photos taken
with iPhones and posted on Facebook.
This is our apocalypse when we trample
with embarrassment, set fire to churches, book burning
with Bibles, copies of Glen Beck's latest, march down
main streets in every town and city: "We're queer.
We're here. Get used to it," for the millionth time.
Toads fall from heaven; apples land
on Newton's head, burying the ignorant
with something to think about,
another eye-opening experience,
Tim Gunn healing the sick ones,
hands flying, advising they "make it work,"
RuPaul singing lullabies, dragging press-on
fingernails over eyelids while each one lies in bed,
and Harvey Milk will rise from the dead, grabbing
our attention, hundreds of thousands of people
listening, his ghost yells into a megaphone,
"If a gay person makes it,
the doors are open to everyone."
The sky turns a certain shade of pink.
Gunshots are heard in the distance.

AN INTROVERT TRAVELS WITH GIFTS

A brown paper shopping bag, actually two
because it's doubled, filled with approximately
twenty books, paperback and hardcover,
a selection for my nephews, niece, and mother,
sitting open as nature allows it, on the floor
between two train seats, exposing my gifts
to other passengers balancing in the aisle;
And I'm a sand person from desert scenes
in *Star Wars* having dropped a satchel
in the beginning of a sci-fi movie, circa mid-1970s,
but now riding a New Jersey Transit train,
traveling away from New York City, waiting
to arrive in the town where my parents live,
to catch a ride to my brother's, a ten-minute drive
from there; all fourth wise man who said he'd meet them
later in Bethlehem, I sit in motion, the fifth wise man
coughing out of control in the aisle seat
across from me. He's way older, overweight,
and possibly suffering from emphysema.
He'll survive this trip, but I've got the bag,
the gift for those I worship. I want to raise my club,
scare visitors on this otherworldly desert,
totally not their planet, swing it like a fly swatter,
trying to kill an angel, shreds of sand-colored cape,
wraparound robe slapping arms and faces.
It's sci-fi all the way, another ride out of the city,

bittersweet safety, an elderly camel beneath me,
still capable but moaning. The joy of seeing family,
sharing prizes from a job in publishing.
I wish I could travel in a rocket ship instead,
solo and glowing, a bright, bright star,
then crash land in a barn far from home.

DEAD BY DAWN

Visible paths in water, some bay at home
on the coastline, near black and tinted green:
a city of vamps rinsing Starry Night hair dye
in a manmade lake, once clear and clean.
Maybe speedboats traveled past, invisible hands
pushed plastic toys in bathtubs, like some monster
infant sitting in this—legs spread, each under
an arch of the raised train tracks, the ones
I'm traveling on, and it's close to seven,
nighttime in late summer. People go boating
by the Jersey shore. The water is something to stare at.
Who wants to see how many grays exist, how dull
the city is on a Sunday early evening? The bath water
seems distant, sitting in a tub foreign. The alarm clock
should be set, time needed for a shower, a path to make
in the morning, footsteps over wreckage, hurricane leftovers,
a child's temper tantrum made driftwood out of row boats.
Every minute toward the front door, another hair falls
from the head; it's Monday again, goddamn it—
surviving vamps wander in robes, twisted towels—
soak everything in coffee and drown.

1993

Stretched rectangle, classic candy-cane
red-and-white stripes, even, slanted,
twenty feet of Christmas wrapping paper
pasted between "Danger—No Clearance" signs.
Someone spray-painted "1993" left of center,
and a woman in a brown three-quarter length coat,
topped with a paisley scarf, steps closer to the M train,
held at the station, and knocks on closed doors,
like "open sesame" happens for blonde white women
in gentrifying neighborhoods. Who thinks of doing that,
let alone taking action? And did a guy jump down
from the platform, late-night one early '90s evening
to date this place, leave a mark while risking life or limb?
I wish it weren't raining and a stranger hadn't dropped an umbrella,
some alarm louder than opened doors at Essex, a knee-drumming
twentysomething in glasses, baseball cap, jeans, and Converse.
Exit at Chambers, walk to a staircase that leads to the 6 train,
following people, downed poles on roadways, live wires hiss
and slap asphalt, underground and too slow of a pace
for me late to meet my sponsor, another Starbucks
to discuss character defects. Thirteen years clean
and still a struggle to not shove strangers
who enter the train before you exit,
to wish missed footfalls next step up,
arms circling, row-boat oars panicked,
total fall backward trapped in a trust exercise—

no one there to catch you or call for an ambulance.
Spring semester, '93, my freshman year of undergrad,
I came out and tried cocaine at Club USA, 47th Street.
And I'm repeating the Serenity Prayer, avoiding knives out,
six pairs of legs, all younger, seated, nothing but smartphones.
I think of a New Year's Eve, after that Christmas
back in Jersey, sick with fever and a sore throat, suffer hard
each swallow, coughed-on candy canes, family and fuck
this shit. My friends and I smoked crack in a hotel room.
Pajamas under sweat-soaked blankets forgotten,
blood on white tissues used to catch sneezes,
clean sheets covering the physically torn apart,
a young man on subway tracks, limbs connected
by rubber bands. We watched the ball drop,
then snorted bags of heroin; another year
welcomed, whichever one, it didn't matter.

WE GO TOGETHER

Another text from my brother—"still no power"—
a week since the superstorm, circular photos of Sandy
from the *Grease* movie expanding from Florida up the East Coast,
a graphic on Facebook, shared and commented on: Olivia Newton-John
in stages, Sandra Dee with bangs switching to makeup made-up face
all vixen and topped with blonde and curly, one with mouth open—
out to destroy New York City, do her number in moonlight,
surge high with high-heeled jumps, stretching black spandex,
hormones shift and seize, causing thighs and ass cheeks
to flex more with bent knees, like kicking the shit out of sand castles
or dancing on a grave, the murderer of your child or the rapist
who never went away; she fled the carnival in the final scene, graduation
free-for-all, ending the song and tearing free from celluloid, jacked
on meth, all "Where am I?" mugshot, scratched face sores,
seaweed tangled and almost drowned, just chewed
free from Jaws, trailing shark intestines, bloodied
death grip on the Jersey shore. I saw a photograph
the day after, the way-submerged roller coaster
at Seaside, the missing boardwalk, smashed tables
in a bar fight, wreckage dragged by the Atlantic, and
I don't remember riding it the multiple times visited,
only buying tickets at a booth, five or four for entry,
the Octopus cars would spin over water,
waves approaching the shoreline—I feared
accidents, my ride detaching, launched all Frisbee,
dead on impact with the sea. And scenes turned ugly,

moon, water, and wind continuing a bar crawl, fistfights
on Hoboken streets, meatheads flying through air,
crashing into trees in every town. A ConEd plant exploded
in Lower Manhattan, the fireworks to celebrate global warming,
the pop pop my coworkers heard, footage from Long Island City,
subway tunnels flooded floor to ceiling, Sandy finger-fucking,
knees high over us, hypnotized by her hand movement, the surge
of wet, her breathing harder than what we imagined, lunar dazed
and coming down, her O-shaped finale, heels gut beach fronts,
dark crashing, more than a hundred deaths already reported.

SOMETIMES SATANIC

The crocheted wool scarf from my ex
too tight on my neck. A girl's mitten tossed
toward an older boy. A leg stretches out
to the center of the walkway in the subway car.
A guy in his late twenties, shaved head and a beard,
with a pushed-back black fedora, like stolen from
a businessman circa 1960, his entire hairline showing
over his stare, a catatonic living in a hospital-room chair,
and I can't help looking although in a relationship,
watching past passersby, the guess of focus—
my unread book and exact location, the don't flinch
when fingertips approach open eyes. He drinks iced coffee,
a shallow box of donuts atop his somewhat spread thighs,
I pull gray and black from beneath my chin,
the design fated by a dye pattern,
the last gift from my ex-boyfriend.
It's a bit warmer out than I had hoped for.
I consider staring back, a single lady
who rules the typing pool, breasts in bullet bra,
angora breathing. Eyes meeting and then a smirk,
very Satan on one shoulder or holding out a document
to sign in blood; perhaps possessed, some goat-haired beast
clicking hooves under bent knees, yanking my pants down,
floor-piled circling my ankles, invisible overgrown fingernails,
tips sharpened, tracing ten lines from ass crack to pale tense hips.
I'm spread in public, bent over, and entered—

a spit-covered force pressing prostate
and traveling in spasms up spine.
My eyes roll back; sight now glitter in the beam
of a flashlight; tongue points at hunted, now detached
and longer, the run-over's insides bursting paint-splat all over,
directed at the fly of his pants, button swallowed, underwear over it,
bitten and teased, some nocturnal sniffing tents at a campsite,
then pawing at the odor, mouth open. The boy stands and kicks;
the girl whips her scarf, an unfolded apron for pretend
I'm baking, and "mother" is shouted in Spanish.
Back to my book, forgetting the wool pulled close,
choke hold on a warm winter day, the stink of sulfur
sticking to my hair and coat, the sweat
around my asshole, the devil leaked out.

WHAT'S YOUR DAMAGE?

Fifty degrees out, January: I need to blow my nose.
Heathers on Showtime last night; I watched more
than half, very basement in my parents' house,
ninth grade, me and two friends on a leather couch.
And they played hopscotch in grammar school,
while I jumped rope in another playground,
where boys called me faggot
and picked me last in gym.
And I threw one down a hill,
his body a stunt double,
messy dive through a window,
like in an '80s horror movie—
when killers chucked corpses to shatter glass
and get closer. He smacked my head for no good reason,
so I pictured a jump rope around his neck and kitchen knives
in backpacks. I'd stab like beating out a fire, very Manson member
following orders, nothing like Michael Meyers jamming a knife,
a young man left fixed to a wall, like a reminder on a cork board.
And Veronica mixes milk with orange juice
in Heather's kitchen, her vengeance
for being asked, "What's your damage?";
called a cooze for being so high school,
puking in a hallway at a Remington party.
They want Heather to vomit the morning after.
Christian Slater's character fills a mug with rust remover.
Veronica makes a mix up, waking Heather with the wrong cup.

"You think I'll drink it just because you call me chicken."
Never looking inside, Heather adds,
"Just give me the cup, jerk."
Then gagging, throat clutching
before the classic "Corn nuts,"
spoken half a second previous to her free fall in pink,
face forward atop a coffee table; tempered glass explodes
outward, granular chunks land voodoo-dust circle
trapping new dead. Three ninth-graders
laughed because it's only a movie;
we smiled at acted-out scenes
of popular students being murdered.
I'm waiting for a J train and it's warm for January.
I'm stuck on *Heathers,* jocks stripped to underwear
and shot in the woods, this shit didn't happen
in either small town I grew up in:
boxers and briefs, bullet holes in chests.
And once I squeezed a sharpened pencil
in freshman math class, considering it halfway deep
in the back of a classmate after he turned and said faggot
before pushing a book off my desk. Boys being boys,
hand flying, closed fist knocking a locked door,
choose your favorite on-screen serial killer
approaching very speed walker.
Jamie Lee Curtis screaming,
"Let me in!" Punctures for real,
Heather's not breathing,
his blood on my desk, like Manson-style finger writing,
and I was red, face flushed, noticed stares from peers

possibly concerned—students claiming to have known
Heather when she was alive. My hand opened.
The pencil rolled across my test paper.
"Fuck me gently with a chainsaw."
Remember that line in the cafeteria.

NEVER GO DOWN AND CAUSE FIRES

The MTA warns, "Never go down on the tracks."
The reason given: "If you drop something";
as though no others existed, like collecting litter
or suicide, lying across, a horizontal line in a table,
column heads typed above you. iPhones are expensive,
pointless if the owner's limbs are dragged from a torso,
brain matter coating tracks, human cells scattered
beaten open piñata, fullest trash bag of garbage
tossed in front of an A train—express, on time,
the everyday appearance below the platform:
organ systems unraveled, empty plastic bottles,
ripped shopping bags, the red ones used in Chinatown,
so many hanging from hands at Canal, catch the J, M, or Z,
but step aside because courtesy is contagious; let the passengers
off first, and litter on the tracks can cause fires. More cases
this fall of strangers pushed off platforms, pretty much murdered.
Loud talk during a fire drill—time to separate those two.
A man with his back to the wall, another shouting
in his face; he's considered this for years, the garbage
below him, how rats run when in danger, the way
the train sounds when entering the station.

BANG BANG BEHIND AN AQUARIUM

He asked her if it was just bang bang,
sitting behind me on a NJ Transit train.
I guess that's not dating a mutual friend
but sex here and there, needs filled,
fucking on a couch in a furnished basement,
the unprotected splitting halves on cushions,
wet opening battered, a marsupial pouch fisted
behind a fifty-gallon aquarium, football trophies
on shelves built into walls, displayed since childhood,
his baby arm pounding a drum, lodged pink deep,
a diaphragm for birth control but she's on the pill.
It's just his hips against her bottom: bang bang
they say, like gun shots in the Outback,
kangaroos wiping out face first,
buckshot in hides, wet spots,
stains on upholstery. He doesn't ask
how often this happens, but says do what
you want to do. Three more stops and I'm out
of here. Music not loud enough played from an iPod,
a new term overheard, and it's not yet St. Patrick's Day,
the parade happening, couches waiting for company,
all floors in houses or apartments outside of the city,
dinner at Outback, rare steak and lobster tail,
no salad, the pink inside bleeding on a plate,
something pulled limp from a pouch, dead joey.

Bang bang he said. Her legs still spread.
She's leaking an aquarium of hungry fish.

HAND WASH

following a Wayne Koestenbaum reading at the New School, April 17, 2013

New School bathrooms where healthy hand washing
is promoted, instructions in numbered steps,
listed in an uncommon font and posted eye-level
to the right of the sink, and this is not the men's room
I remember: tall marble walls between stalls, simply not
scrawled on, but used to see into, past the curves
in black marker, built backs, buttocks, naked men
cartooned and exaggerated, in-shape gay bikers
lifted from '70s man on man, films and photo spreads,
the kind who wear leather jackets over bare torsos.
A pair somewhere left sideline-entertainment seeming
permanent, one's mid-cock a high-powered telescope
dropped stories, now half-buried in the other's hole,
ass cheeks spread to a flat surface punched through,
the bottom pinned down, inside him examined, some lens
in his colon, this fucking more like fisting, the stretch
impossible, like power lifter past the elbow, see it,
touch it, what makes the peed-through grow,
drawn man on his back, open-mouth imagined moan
beneath a '70s gay biker mustache, eyes closed
more sun bather on the beach than trying to force sleep
or not see a limb severed in a gore-fest horror movie.
Scene circled in perv commentary, requests for more,
phone numbers, meet me at this time, pants down,
walls where the New School must have remodeled,

no more turn-on between marble, ass-down and hardening,
seeing through these make-believe men, their permanent
pleasure, the hand washing done to clean away semen,
cum, smudges of marker. The in-wall urinals
I recall not using, porcelain-bottom canoes upright
flooding top to bottom, replaced by gutted eggs,
2001 urinals, what set designers in the '60s
imagined men in space pissing in, the nostalgia
of a public bathroom, rumored hot house
for academic homos, college students
jerking off before class, just stop here
and wash your hands, it's no longer
embarrassing, more posthumous,
stared through, new school,
classic and dead.

STRAYS

Starlings eat cat food off the sidewalk,
kibbling on Styrofoam plates, last night's
leftovers scattered by local strays.
A woman in a raincoat offers it,
water as well in washed-out plastic,
containers that held ricotta cheese or yogurt.
Guests gone home, no cleaning service hired,
daily street festivals, house parties filter overflow
out a front door, homeless celebrating
fresh food found in a dumpster,
malnourished children fed
by missionaries. She bends over,
hand extended toward faces, an initial sniff
before fingers spread attempting to touch fur,
pat heads. Some will approach, although
you're not her, late at night, walking home—
everyone knows where they're heading.
Their lives assisted, the homeless
capable at city living, no change lost
from paper cups, every quarter edible,
adding together. Those not domesticated,
born outdoors, like starlings hatched in nests,
the kind between buildings, three-floor residences;
inhabitants hear them, calls of newborns
forced free, sitting in egg shells.
The stray cats are hiding, gifts shared;

they leave messes, saliva-smudged glasses,
empty pill bottles in medicine cabinets,
silverware on crumb-covered tables,
remnants of a past on Styrofoam plates.

BLACK AND WHITE

A dead guinea pig in a shoebox, black and white and matted,
set on the sidewalk, lid off, outside the methadone clinic,
closer to the corner, the crosswalk, beneath aboveground tracks
for the JMZ, where I walk every weekday morning, keeping
the 9 to 5, distance from smokers at 8:15, coming or going
to or from a full or an empty plastic cup on a counter
and someone standing behind a window with four sides,
boxlike but filled with life, the opposite of curled,
fur-covered claws permanently raised near chest,
two toothpick-sized shepherd canes glued to a body,
a hair ball coughed up, black and white and greasy,
that started in a trash can or a knotted-closed bag of garbage,
ripped open by a stray cat. His or her paws reached in, removed,
exhumed, sent this former pet feet across the sidewalk,
the dead for another ride, the kill that didn't happen, limbs intact,
no bite marks. No one else is staring at it. Does anyone ever
get used to this? The addicts still hooked, no longer shooting
up, talk like blocks apart while smoking their cigarettes.
They appear in color, the dullest hues possible—four walls
following them, somehow coughed up, walking, one foot
in a shoebox, the homeless woman in Starbucks, the businessman
dancing while in line for coffee, all stuffed inside like garbage,
the music in his headphones, street cats stare at shapes from outside
a trash bag, a black-and-white guinea pig is dead on the sidewalk.

INCREDIBLE HULK

An empty Sprite can side down
on a subway seat, shiny green leftover
of someone lazy, the Hulk's middle finger
severed and laminated.
He was gray in his earliest appearances,
kind of zombie flesh, what aged dead looks like,
in the first comic-book panes fought through.
And it's moved to the floor,
nothing spilled out,
no puddle to avoid sitting in—I always look
first, because you never know what's down there,
like leaks from adult diapers appearing as sweat,
wet being better late
and heading home, but cry worthy
at 8:28 a.m., still sleepy despite a cup of coffee,
when you fear turning green gripping a horizontal pole
overhead so squeezed
like meat hooked and hanging, a frozen slab
of steer inside a slaughterhouse freezer, so much
showing in public, an empty glass bottle
finished rolling against
your foot. And Hulk smash everything,
fists like sledgehammer heads, larger than watermelons;
when bad things happen to good people, a herd
of walking dead crowding you,
mouths open and moaning, two step on your toes.

The subway doors close, more peaceful tonight,
my forehead cooler, air-conditioned,
the Sprite can rolls away
seeking another's company.

ON PREFERRING UNSCENTED

She moisturizes her hands seated on a J train,
approaching the bridge to enter Manhattan,
and I'm grateful it's not a strong scent,
someone in the office cleaning his or her desk
with something floral out of a spray bottle,
unlike running through a field of lavender,
more like coffin-side at a wake,
Catholic and open casket,
flowers arranged potted and on stands,
each the size of outdoor shrubs at corners of lawns
or an aged staghorn fern hanging in a tree, in heart shapes
and circles or simple bushlike blobs, smelling of misery,
all good things come to an end. Her dry hands
in August, maybe she washes tons of dishes,
her summer shorts set covered by an apron.
The possibility of a minimum-wage job,
her white skin, blonde hair, a high-fashion purse,
the kind you find knockoffs of
around Times Square or Canal Street.
And her fingers rub up and down in heat-me-up motions;
the palms wrapping over the tops like aggressive hand washing,
as though just finished gardening, the earth from the lifeline,
what's stuck under the nails, the decline of skin, downhill
from here—she may get buried under flowers in the end.

SPACED OUT

People tend to crowd at the ends of subway trains,
even when the floor stretches past poles and feet
of the seated, a rolled-out map of an unknown universe,
where stars come in white and red, clotting the black
background like too many shells washed up on a beach—
you can't fly through this or walk on it, somewhere
planets exploded and we were unaware,
like there are more fragments to balance on,
floating out by the seats for two, by doors
to the next car; no seat belts to buckle in,
keep us safe during space travel, explore
old school, like we're cruising across
a flat world, our sails flying squirrels
stretched in sky dive, four claws,
one for each corner, attached
to wood poles: getting somewhere,
as though this train is really angled upward,
passengers still upright beyond take off, but slid
toward the down end, a handful of Jackson moonwalkers—
how did they do that? I cut my tether every time and take
barefoot steps on broken shells, seek the empty black
blanket no one seems to walk on, space in this city,
even on the subway, unknown galaxy easily reached,
where aliens were vaporized, their red-and-white insides,
stains on the fabric, so similar to humans but unique.

RUNNERS LOVE GHOSTS

Let's get blank, like worn out after a marathon,
the morning after a night in, cooking rocks
at the end of a glass stem, shot-gunning hits
with your new best friend, the lack of the erotic
when lips touch and his exhale is inhaled,
a man-made ghost losing matter lungs deep,
my last-step breath—a gravity-free vomit,
cloud-shaped insides float to the ceiling.
We discuss the closeness of the police station,
across the street and past your closed curtains:
blankets nailed to walls covering the windows.
And a finish line appears, as though hallucinated;
the invisible pull it tight across the road, like trees
are participating, woodland critters one atop the other,
totem poles alive behind trunks, branches—some claws
involved, holding loose corners. You claimed my car's
headlights were alien eyes, worried over Herbie for real
but extraterrestrial. And I didn't laugh; I believed you.
I suggested you stop peeking out the windows, to forget
the possibility my Dodge Neon can blink, because it's time
to count our money so we can keep running, the finish line
moved a hundred feet, our blank space spreading,
the glass stem recently used frying-pan hot,
my lips a touch burnt. Ghosts warm
by the ceiling; we need to take off.

THIS IS CALLED MAKING IT

With a canvass tote from Spandex World hung over
the shoulder, she and her comrade carry clothing
in folded traveling hanger bags, the zip-up kind
people transport suits and dresses in to avoid
wrinkling. These two fashion designers,
young enough to have just graduated from FIT
or Parsons, their outfits a step up in shine, construction,
from other local Bushwick artists, like pants, jacket,
white blousy button-down sewn at home, patterned
first while turning pages of the September issue.
Their stretched garment dreams visible, pulled over
thighs, hips, the better to dress the rich in, bodies
where the money is. The avant-garde historically
too expensive for Bohemia: the writers, painters,
dancers, the costume designers, found-junk sculptors,
printmakers, performance artists acting out
near the closest Korean market. And some program,
scene, or episode is being filmed beneath the tracks
on Broadway in Brooklyn, all these folks at the corners
wearing head sets or holding walkie-talkies.
Maybe the new season of *Girls* happening here
in my neighborhood; months later I'll watch it on HBO,
see why cable is so expensive, two TVs, one DVR.
And this is middle class, unlike starting out
and twenty-something, folks stuck on stability—
a 9-to-5 job to pay New York City rent and songs

written in spare time, band practice on weekends,
the poet using the Notes app on his iPhone to keep up,
take advantage of wasted time riding the subway, sitting
on stairs outside the post office at 34th and 8th, early
to meet friends for dinner on a Tuesday night, working
toward a second full-length collection, outside of being
a production editor at a large publishing house in Manhattan.

COLOR ME BORED, 2014

I want to smudge her face, mix colors like sides
and destroyed entree on a plate, not caused by
misogynistic instincts, but because she's wearing
too much makeup, looking fashion model,
early 1980s, posing for a *Vogue* cover
like a colored-in Nagel, pastels and charcoals abused
until lifelike, the features not the tools, just sitting there
with headphones staring at an iPad, blinking
every so often and traveling to Brooklyn.
And no reason is involved, it's just Hump Day
snowing nonstop throughout work hours, daytime,
slippery sidewalks and subway staircases dealt with
and crowded on the train, the result of near blizzard,
no one bicycling across the bridge.
Dead passion again at early evening,
approaching forty and one stop closer
to home, looking down on her, them, those
sitting—really because I'm standing: tall, upright,
classical, a marble statue in a hallway
of the Metropolitan Museum, except out of shape
and dressed for the office. She's using a program
to create music on her tablet, just like my boyfriend
mixing beats, adding guitar, bass.
The overweight woman on her left
watches the screen over her shoulder,
some underpaid employee leaning on a wall

waiting to tell a patron "no photos please."
All the curiosity, the so close together, a line
at the supermarket waiting in the express lane,
we look at the *Vogue* covers, the new issues of *Cosmo*
and *Vanity Fair*—fifteen items or less—the fashion models
no longer reminiscent of colored-in Nagels, cleaned-off
plates over the garbage pail, today we recycle old magazines;
although some people collect them, post scanned covers online,
and this year it really feels like winter, dry skin, hot breath,
the face-washing in a cold apartment while showering
or standing in front of a sink full of water,
the mirror steamed up, colors still visible.

GAY VIKINGS IN LOVE

Awesome, Babe, you and me against the world.
Too bad we couldn't leave the same time for work;
although I'm aware your lyrics are not literal,
entirely us in the physical, battle axes raised,
Viking helmets worn tilted, monsters on the horizon
a football field away, drunk frat boys at a toga party
or shirtless and painted at a stadium in Minnesota.
That song you play at shows, the one titled "Baby,"
with guitar unlacing the front of me, like opening
a corset, a flesh-tone one keeping contents inside,
your voice through the microphone, extra reverb,
I'm a Voodoo doll, claimed and spellbound,
fan girl front and center, closest to the stage.
Me and you against the world, lovebirds on rocket fuel,
two bullets through a thousand hearts, blood trails drag
from sidewalk traffic, animated birds carrying a banner
beaks clasped at corners; "Always be mine,"
printed in red cursive letters. And here I am:
stitched up, conscious on a surgeon's table,
the end of the song, the stairs to the J train.
My battle axe is raised, Babe. I'm prepared
to swing it, because we're together,
thousands of drunks loud in a stadium,
a pin through my heart, our love
loud and furious.

DOWNTOWN READING ON A RAINY DAY

Inspired at someone else's poetry reading, all the mouths
moving—the loudest at the podium, as it should be.
All of us celebrating seated and paying attention,
men pacing on subway platforms with backpacks
hanging low like adjustable straps were too hard
to manage each half a minute stepping on yellow,
the foot-and-a-half warning of the edge, and peeking in
the black of a slightly lit tunnel, counting in footsteps
for the next door to open. Some rub tops of thighs
attempting to dry damp denim, hoping the dye
from this new unwashed pair hasn't stained legs
like bear attacked from the waist down,
or better yet, trapped in a doggie door,
the lower half outside at some gorilla sanctuary,
and an older male silverback pummeling the lengths
of what is available, the once bendable only at the knees
while seated at a poetry reading, waiting for a favorite,
a hero in all this other poet's time frames, the call
of the wild, let's beat the shit out of the weakest
among us. Let's hear another poem about poets
getting catty, these mouths worthwhile, black jeans
drying in an art space; wet again waiting for the J train.

WHEN POETS ATTACK

Come on with those tight track pants.
Your ride the D; mine the M. It's been insects
and sparrows in Bryant Park, dry leaves in summer
somehow crumbling against thighs, upper arms,
beneath black skinny jeans and a plum polo shirt,
a reenactment of Pacific battles from World War II,
birds close to the reader's head, chasing one another,
songs over oceans, war calls, outdoors,
this nighttime poetry reading
with audience seated on hard folding chairs.
Masked sparrows hopping after landing, words through
loud speakers, not enemies or friends. People pass by,
walking paths on either side of somewhere called
the Reading Room, this event space,
and they swat at moving dots
illuminated at few spots in city dark,
what we accept. But they only watch,
attracted to a crowd and an announcer-loud voice,
an invite to join, take a seat. And I consider rock throwing,
primeval weaponry, hurting the unwilling and free,
the every day it's summer,
this night is made for walking, new creatures
like born again, adults baptized in lakes, travelers in Manhattan
preferring to stare at skyscrapers, not everyone gets poetry,
round man-ass in gray below a loose tank top,
the just sat through seven poets

and feeling extra sensitive, half-hard inside
twisted underwear, warmth begs for sweaty hands,
another evening in the city, saved by words, common birds,
an explosion overhead, holy moments beneath burning leaves.
Gray stretched when he entered a subway train.
Rocks not thrown, invites ignored, it's been
insects and sparrows in Bryant Park.

SATAN SAYS FUCK THE FIRST HOT PIECE OF ASS YOU SEE ON THE SUBWAY

"Always on My Mind" done with orchestral instruments,
underground through headphones, the young man's eye contact
with this older stranger. He's current, wearing the latest
in men's fashion, cross-country flights from rubber sandals,
the kind with Nike swooshes, worn with socks and basketball shorts
loose and long. The foreign and familiar, I don't know you
but I know what you want, a short trip in the air from one island
to another, under a spell after playing a metal record backward.
A force like "walk on, water's on the other side of the mountain,"
goats in a farmhouse to choose from. Something says drink, look,
sacrifice at nighttime, Satan on a loudspeaker. *Always on my mind,
tell me*—one more chance to keep you satisfied, follow fashion,
the next stop you move for the exit, a path of goat blood
to a stranger's apartment, much prettier in the nude,
an instrumental that never ends,
a thirst vanquished, one man
inside another.

COLD LIFE OVER YOUNG CHINS

I don't want this century, the majority of my life
lived in it. The graffiti on a rooftop wall, viewed
while crossing the Williamsburg Bridge:
a spring green alien shaped like squash,
the top half extending from a corner, dot eyes
and smiling; "summertime loves mischief 2013,"
in thinly sprayed print, all lowercase.
No fireflies here or rectangles of lawn
along the sides of two-family houses
that curve partway around the front
to meet a driveway, perennial flowers
planted by grandfathers presented like an audience,
a standing ovation, alive in an L of soil, cheering
at the bottom of cement steps leading outside
from a front door, the last quarter of the twentieth century,
the camera held to the eye and holding film, the say cheese
and a serious flash at the start of sundown. And who remembers
the Shmoo? A character in a 1980 Saturday morning cartoon,
an all white bowling pin that smiles, blinks, changes shape
at will, a snowman destroyed then rebuilt a hundred times
in five minutes or less, a flattened block of vanilla ice cream
rolled into a ball, what fits in a cone, something thought of
in summer, sucking at the bit-off tip, sticky wet in thin drips,
cold life over young chins, lips, another night
in the backyard, fireflies everywhere,
towels soaked in pool water hung over fences.

I'm 2013, a digit on a train, aimed at Manhattan,
at home, regardless, each year alien, faces I see
in every direction, the bed of flowers I fell in,
the day I stop caring. It's winter.
I'm forty. It's all so amazing.

PART II
IN WITH THE NEW

WE GO SEASONAL

There's no Santa Claus and we all die—
and this is eleven. Two candles Twin Towers parallel,
mimicking the number of this age another Christmas,
torches in ice cream cake, a sparking tuning fork,
buried handle-first in ground a touch still frozen.
My nephew's birthday and he's a year older.
He reminds me he was born at 5:23. His mother
told him once and it somehow stuck.
I never asked my mom that question or if I did
it's entirely forgotten, unlike spring weather
every shared birthday cake with my grandmother,
the day before, after, or of Mother's Day, each candle
a maypole, pagan and danced around, each year
things changing, underarms and voices,
so much to look forward to, life to celebrate,
candles blown out to applause, making a wish,
a cloud of soot exploding from the fireplace,
a chain of flowers left dying in the dirt.

SLIP'N SLIDE

Creative types lubricate it all,
bend dangerous ways, capable,
untrained in contortion,
elastic folk pretzeled on lawns,
supporting what comes next,
consolation prizes for living—
trophies learn to walk, run, your DNA
unaware of oncoming traffic, what wheels do
on roads to toddlers recently experiencing
on two feet, the first hundred footsteps
toward doing what comes natural
and what is learned, an adult hand
hooking the back of a crew-neck collar
so fast it hurts to red-on-skin still-so-new
and you move backward and off the ground,
like dads sucked vacuum-cleaner-up from outside
open doors of basements as the last child is dumped
down with mom as a twister passes taking him and
the farm, and there goes a car—you'll always remember
air moving everywhere, falling off a diving board while
facing the sky, like antigravity, better than a jump
on a trampoline. You're DNA in motion, praise-
worthy, bending legs, arms, as far as possible,
still red with pain but unable to stop walking.

SOME BIRDS ARE SMARTER THAN OTHERS

A starling runs down a driveway into a parking garage
on a wet day in winter, rain continues since dark out
and a blind finger found a square button, topside
of an alarm clock. A quiet December drizzle allows
no clues prior to a shower; this isn't monsoon like,
and somehow the temperature rose to forty,
no cars encased in thin sheets of ice, mostly clear,
like Willy Wonka's new candy shells: examine the filling
and guess the flavor. Maybe the most simple will turn
your insides out, lead you to a van with no windows,
a blindfolded ride that starts out soaked-rag unconscious.
Tastes the dirt you're buried in, behind the local factory.
This rain keeps at it, and puddles join forces;
pedestrians drop bombs in high seas,
attempt to sink battleships. Umbrellas pass
butter-the-bread, children cross underwater,
one top, one bottom, a swimming-pool game.
A toe may touch a back, air bubbles decorate,
spin like light shows in see-through tunnels,
and no other birds land sidewalk excited,
drinking or splashing, not even the pigeons.

I'M NOT MAD AT YOU;
I'M MAD AT THE DIRT

My mother said, "You're breathing that stuff in."
I couldn't remember when I last cleaned
the top of the refrigerator. Tonight I used
half a roll of paper towels, maybe just a third,
the spray bottle of kitchen cleaner back under
the sink. Months of dust rolled like wet bath towels,
some microscopic pool house, well-stocked cabana,
smashed by King Kong fists angry at rooftops, the slants
of enemies. Off from work for the holidays
and I haven't scrubbed the bathtub
and I never put a tree up,
close to six months since Dad died,
I have a whole suitcase full of Christmas lights;
my grandmothers' ornaments are stored in boxes
in the living room closet, a shelf where things get dusty,
that furniture covered with white sheets in those movies
where things happen in abandoned houses
or summer homes forgotten. It's hairy this season,
a monster unchained, pounding the top of my refrigerator,
the tiniest water-logged bath mats stuck to tile flooring,
each day of the month, a miniature dead lightbulb.
My mother's right about that stuff:
breathing it all in.

HELL MOUTH ENDS IN GREEN

Evil Dead 2 projected on a curtain behind the first band on stage,
the main character starts cutting his hand off with a chainsaw;
his mouth and eyes open to their limits, the expression you'd expect
out of torture. And her brother has a snowboard. A guy in a hoodie
standing near me said so. He's telling the woman to his right
that they'll need to buy ski lift tickets. It's in between songs,
human mutilation, the action on stage bordered by a clear tube
filled with lights that change color, a magical garden hose nailed
to the edge facing the audience, a stretched earthworm alive
with electricity, a ski-lift cable allowing colors to drag
for our eyes only. Somebody's brother is speeding
down a mountainside this moment or next week,
and it's all Ash from *Evil Dead 2* chasing his severed hand
in an abandoned cabin in a forest; the band is starting a new song,
now lit red from below, a thousand glass marbles carrying blood,
rolling through the longest drinking straw, blood cells illuminated
through skin by a flashlight pressed to one side of a flatter appendage
or held bright end to open mouth, cheeks stretched like a pair
of projector screens closing in on an entrance to hell,
what torture can do to lips pulling against teeth
during the loudest scream, the last song
from the stage, a skier launched headfirst
into a tree. Earthworms digging farther;
the light turns green.

NEVERLAND GETS CROWDED

The reaction is uh-oh when approached in winter by a crowd,
some group on a mission to not lose one another because it is
a big city, these schools of fish dodging the toothiest mouths,
the darkness where tongues can't possibly exist,
the field-trip-happy mass of students visiting
this street or that, Times Square, Rockefeller Center,
the crowded molars, incisors, and others left unattended
after their owner stopped wearing a retainer to keep it all
straight, the bottom one flushed down a toilet during a black out,
the top one too tight to fit thanks to bad habits, neglect of hygiene.
And the subway system is celebrating one hundred ten years in existence,
as old as some towns in New Jersey, the street where the orthodontist
was located, his office decorated for children, what that meant
in the mid-1980s, the two years promised to visit monthly,
orange cabinets and white desktops and counters,
the receptionist who wore her hair teased,
the assistant still feathered, long.
The women on Broadway, our walk
toward Radio City Music Hall, a little hand
squeezed by his mother's, a choked python's head,
Chinese finger trap, already close to a slightly bent wrist.
Sandy Duncan is playing Peter Pan in a limited engagement.
The theater seats in rows, children and parents, uh-oh inside
when we stand on velvet-covered cushions, get closer
to the farthest-away-ever ceiling, the arc over

six thousand open mouths, tongues showing.
It's a lead up to a slow black out,
crowds no longer moving.

CLOSE ENCOUNTERS

Some summer days close to noon, the hour or two that follow,
a circular section of a backyard appears landing-pad eerie,
grass flattened like this was a campsite, what tents did,
bodies inside them. And there once was a pool here,
above ground, filled and chlorinated, water in motion,
splashes over rails, a pot stirred too fast, children swimming
follow-the-leader close to walls, around nonstop—whirlpool.
Pros at this, having learned to swim, days of tossed upward
by dads starting to lose shape, gain weight, and their exercise
of lifting sons and daughters until biceps burn, how high
do you want to go—the launch of blue-collar arms,
bent to straight out, the up there over water,
wearing a red-and-white striped life jacket,
skydive without a parachute, how high
does fifty pounds travel, a half-second
memory, the effect sought on trampolines
years later at gymnastics class, that quest
for gold, whatever the future holds, the arms out
and mouth wide open, missteps on fell dead trees
over deep rushing rivers, slip and land lost, head fully
underwater. It's another good day on summer vacation,
the grass green, and great aunts with hair in rollers,
wearing sunglasses and a one-piece bathing suit,
watch from a lounge chair, back up,
rubbing baby oil on chest, arms, and legs.
And the older kids swim in circles, a grandmother yells,

"Be careful!" recalling her son-in-law dislocating
her granddaughter's shoulder
when lifted too fast, hand in hand,
rough palms of a blue-collar worker,
the patience of a summer day, impossible to remove
that sweaty T-shirt, get up the deck staircase he built
with a niece's husband with a background in carpentry.
The great aunt lights a cigarette, reclining far from poolside,
closer to the chain-link fence, the neighbors and their actions.
Some summer afternoons, wind felt on a less humid day
where an above-ground pool once stood behind
a two-family house, bodies inside it, where
someone else's family once lived, something
eerie about this spot in the grass, flattened
like a flying saucer landed here,
then carried them all away.

WE DO HOSPITALS AND LEAVE

I have to label this river, watch another disaster movie,
speak to boys in mint green jammies seated on pleather couches,
I mean, you know, really tell them my story, sweep the side roads,
the kind Google maps can't offer street views of, the walkways
to front yards where dead daffodils still stand in late spring,
the eyesores of white petals turning brown to black,
burnt edges of one sheet of typing paper, the circle of them
planted around a light post, the painted to match the shutters,
where they hung the address number of the house, two digits
on a piece of metal cut in the shape of a banner, this whole thing
in the way when mowing the lawn. It's a pow wow
in a locked psych ward, a 12-step meeting
on the eighth floor, where someone leads
these in-patients, introduces a speaker
from the outside. One young guy asks
if they like KISS. "You mean like the band.
I fucking love them." Maybe because we're both
dressed in all black, like this must be witchcraft,
hand me the special knife, it's time to feed the earth.
It's time to hire a mapmaker, offer suggestions on how
not to die, like follow me at top speed on foot away from
the nearest body of water. Some goddamn tidal wave
is coming. Don't you know some people
manage to outrun it, always breathing
heavy until the end.

DOOMED HERE

Us surrounded—so alive—
bounce feet to music, sounds funneled
through wire and plastic, milk-colored rubber;
hollow soft teeth fill ears, where others' words
end neighbors' loud talk in a living room,
the language of Charlie Brown's teacher
on any *Peanuts* special, the volume turned down.
Keeping beat in public because it's music,
been there, done that, "if chocolate makes you happy,"[1]
more lyrics—"dear God, I hate myself"[2]—one artist
on repeat, and it's crowds and crowds, children fighting
too close, Rock 'Em Sock 'Em competitors, waist high,
more vocal than adults, a girl whacking a boy's shins
with a royal blue umbrella the size of a five-year-old's femur.
Face next to face, the I don't read lips but he's not even looking,
the head down, chin to chest, what science gathers beneath
long hair, black and straight, witchy everywhere at nap time,
the fainted, the silent, the possibly knocked unconscious.
In dreams a cannibal welcomes us at an open front door,
but in waking it's lunchtime on souls, listen even when
avoiding that episode of *The Twilight Zone* never aired
on television, when you no longer understand
the only language you've ever spoken,

---

[1] From the song "Chocolate Makes You Happy" by Xiu Xiu, on their 2010 album *Dear God, I Hate Myself*.
[2] From the song "Dear God, I Hate Myself" by Xiu Xiu, on their 2010 album *Dear God, I Hate Myself*.

every second an unknown letter,
each toe tap code for "fuck this,"
candy bought at a concession stand,
the quest for a buzz in darkness, the view
from a motorized recliner, the future of
movie theaters spreading from suburbs,
but we're standing so close together,
and who has the energy to judge
one's neighbor. We all look
so angry now, like who gave away
the ending, us motherfuckers
patiently waiting to be friendly.

WE FLOAT LIKE MARSHMALLOWS

The numeric code needed
to unlock the bathroom in Whole Foods
saved on a smartphone, stared at and thought on—
should it stay or should it go. The marsh waters
in the Meadowlands, viewed from Jersey train tracks,
seem awfully close to streets that cross through;
cars look lost on hidden paved roads, like somewhere
farther from Newark, street lights, hour-long drives
to tour swamps backseat on an airboat, watch gators
approach, long-distance sperm advance on an egg,
water so dark you miss so much.
And who knew reptiles ate marshmallows,
floating when tossed off the side of a boat?
And this method of travel so unlike brothers
and their father in a rowboat, the near end
to movement, center of a lake, inch from
bull's-eye inside a laurel wreath, all tree tops
tossed away, a giant's crown, his size—small town.
It's just forest every direction, and maybe we'll drown,
gators lost in upstate New York. We can flail until free,
learn to float facedown. It's time to piss off the side
of a boat or behind a tree back on land, somewhere
to go in an emergency, always knowing
a bag of marshmallows gets you closer
to God, his creatures, an end.

FIREWORKS ARE ILLEGAL IN MY HOME STATE

It's not all that bad, recognizing the worst,
the effects of anxiety on human hands, fingers.
Let's discuss fireworks on the Fourth of July,
how the lead up affects children, their psyches,
like some cake of explosions under a chair,
the numbers of limbs blown chunky across town,
on sidewalks, baseball fields. It's mentioned
that Americans drink the most that weekend,
sacrifice watermelons as punch bowls,
split, gutted, filled with vodka, half a bag
of ice-cubes. We're picking skin away
where a hangnail was freed using teeth.
You bled on your new white pants, summer
after all. It's time to say fuck it, get drunk.
It's not so dark, the worst we have
to offer, the smell of just-lit sparklers,
stronger than a few struck matches
in a half bathroom the size of a linens closet,
pops and bangs visible, human heads exploding.

I'VE GOT MY EYES ON YOU

I watch a Yorkie; he looks at her ass.
She walks the dog; her shorts say
summer. Local pups say hug me;
a woman's bottom stops men.
The human fly upright on two,
the other four legs waving
and clapping—cheers for the booty,
three cheers for "wet," what's on the tip
of his tongue. And footsteps on flypaper
unnoticed, sometimes in oncoming traffic,
legs sucked tar pit eat me, down, down,
stuck on words held together in a stranger's
skintight. Every dog wants me to pet it, to lick
my hands and face; we're not talking hard
here, like gay marriage helping
those who prefer the company
of animals. It's just a buzz back,
my hands on all-five doing push-ups
and climbing under basketball shorts,
thighs like hello horse, every man's gift
a possible dick pic on a tumblr page
where someone only posts the heavy
hitters, the it smells good when
out in the open, trained to
stand up and beg,
a handful of kibbles

tossed in the air, unfed
and panting, whose milkshake
is better than whose, makes you
shake your box of Cracker Jacks,
listen for the prize inside, to reach
in, bare hand sticky, warm tar,
bones at the bottom. Oh
man, stroke my wings
if I stop and stare too.

HOW TO REMAIN ACTIVE IN JULY

When I taste air-conditioning,
scent of an examination room,
waiting to undress,
powder where I sweat;
perfect for the beach, this heat,
reason to step from flip-flops,
approach ocean, talk shit
about sand castles,
toss bread to seagulls.
Office hours like upstate winter,
check out wool sweaters,
fingerless gloves, we type
inside, log cabin, no branches
to burn, dry-mouth furnace,
ball gag recently removed.
This tent on solid, we go
ice fishing, pull socks up
as far as possible, dry
by ten a.m. Lunch date
for sushi, another walk outside.
The drip of humid takes no time;
sun bakes legs in denim, shoulders
ping-pong paddles face up on a table
by a refreshment stand,
three shuffleboard courts,
long gray barges docked

in grass. Too hot to be
barefoot, find wet sand
where surf spreads, sidewalk
always shaded, a restaurant
with the best air-conditioning,
seated again, legs hang off ground,
the exam table and its thin paper,
the smell of sweat and powder,
underarms, taste of salt water,
another's thighs inside,
the bedroom first, perfect
beach weather, dry off
undressed, socks on,
hot and cold after five,
facedown on a mattress,
warm breath on my back.

TAKE ME TO THE RIVER

The Hudson River gets gorgeous past Manhattan,
what looks like green mountains, tropical islands
where cruise ships dock. Passengers stand
on ship-side balconies, question if it's Cuba,
could they dive far enough to make the ocean,
swim like hours since Florida and set a record.
And it's been poolside and sun with your best friend,
her husband, and two daughters; we ate pizza and mussels
at an outdoor circular table. There was pink and purple on towels,
bathing suits. Her younger daughter crouched behind bushes
to play with dirt. The older one reported every move.
I got up to see a mess, where the stretch of grass
surprised me, nearly the size of a Brooklyn backyard;
she made you a birthday cake and it's rocks and live ants.
The hands of a three-year-old in it, a decision to reach, turn pair
of rakes, find the change in temperature, a point where things
seem damp, the underside of an island, a version of land
just floating somehow in the same spot, what a kid
imagines if you show him or her a photo of Cuba
or Aruba from a helicopter that one afternoon
flew a far distance above, like it could be closer
to the sun than a docked cruise ship to palm trees
and sand, the ability to step foot on steady land.
A Sunday in summer, we praise cold pool water,
the beauty of trees crowding by a river.

NO PLACE LIKE HOME

Bare asses at eye level, these men,
the kind we want tongues on, the best angles
of hairy over us, and tonight they circle
a patio table, haunts attracted to a certain piece
of furniture, an apartment-sized orgy of a crowd
in back of a beach-town gay bar in Delaware.
We came in knowing of underwear/jock night,
but being visitors, decided against a first
as a couple, who looks better in open-bottom
briefs, buttocks pressed together, cleavage
bra-squeezed atop a corset, easy warmth of skin eager,
pet dogs pushing paws to couch cushions to close
space between your thighs, their backs, a pair
of hairless cats curled against each other on your lap.
Friends, like we watch *Drag Race* together every Monday,
or acquaintances you expect a hug from, shirtless sometimes,
when getting off a bar stool or spinning on foot from the dark
corner of an average studio–sized dance floor, the kitchen
is wall space, a full-size bed fits beneath two windows.
An older gentleman who greeted us
when we first ordered drinks
sits in an outdoor chair next to us
to smoke a cigarette, discuss Rehoboth Beach
in more detail, his life and ours, and based
on statements about his employer's two homes,
how he follows this boss from one to the other, we question

if he's a butler the moment he returns inside, small quest
for a cocktail, on underwear/jock night in this gay bar
in Delaware. Some skin gets covered, loose shorts
pulled up, fewer bare buttocks eye charts to focus on,
near naked men still séance-circle standing,
occasionally touching the closest, everyone
a medium, some spirit dead-set on communicating,
an attack of thrown voices, past meets present.
We're familiar with these walls, the furniture
spread out, the way your favorite dog
or cat can't help but stay close.

IT'S A RICH MAN'S WORLD

This ABBA documentary causes a new need to discover
the origins of their music, having missed the beginning,
but also what year they released a final album. And what
was that stranger selling for a dollar, scrambling first pigeon
at the scene of dropped crackers, kicked in new directions
with each passing person, but it's night and who can hear
with this traffic. We can't even look at him. It can't be
important. The man in the morning asking for change while
a crowd waits for a signal to walk. He said his stomach hurt,
and he just wanted to eat. But who wants to empty pockets
at times like these, turn inside out repeating "I'm sorry.
I can't help you." Time already against you—
the oldest patron in the park standing in place
dropping breadcrumbs, every wild mouth open
beneath dry hands: squirrels, birds, insects
searching the land. You turn for good.
"The winner takes it all. The loser has to fall."
Who knew ABBA would appear on the television,
their story in interviews, videos, and concert footage.
The path to the closest burial ground, albums from
the seventies arranged in boxes and displayed
on folding tables, sold by a stranger outside
the subway entrance. It's 2015.
We'll never make a difference.

MARSHLAND MERRIMENT

My friend's cable-knit sweater
looks more comfortable, thicker.
One photo out of five
shows a red-breasted robin
clear among berries, a leafless tree.
And it's sixty-four degrees,
despite mid-December.
Children read about muskrats,
a displayed fun fact
where we found bathrooms.
A flat cut-out tall as six feet,
cartooned a la Hanna-Barbera,
preaching its story by an exit,
comic-strip letters above its head—
muskrats can swim fifteen minutes
underwater. The trail through marshlands
now all about seeing one. A three-year-old
wobbles close to water's edge,
costumed in swamp stalks,
dry leaves falling off, theater
curtains, plants grown past
eye level, some beyond tops of heads;
they are all neck and Marge Simpson hairstyles,
burnt out from too much time under hair driers.
The five-year-old twists what she finds
on the ground, sand beige strips,

semi-dead versions of what folks use
for basket weaving. She's making bracelets
that won't stay tied, and her sister is ordered
to back up, again too close to a drop,
solid ground to mud to what water is here,
and we joke that a muskrat, nutria large,
wet face and claws, dressed like Yogi Bear,
will pop Jason Voorhees arms out
the end of *Friday the 13th*,
surprising the last girl
seated in a canoe,
his slow-motion hook
and attempt to drown her.
The robins disappeared
when we weren't looking.
We just can't survive
fifteen minutes underwater.

LET ME HEAR YOUR BODY TALK

The man on his back on a workout mat, bent knees, flat feet,
a triangular tunnel formed by legs, bare and far from smooth,
he pinches the ends of running shorts, two towels dropped
on a hotel floor—amateur bodybuilders embrace in the nude,
two hairy thighs flexing against each other, eye-catching
shapes, indents from still fading tan into paler crawl spaces,
hot rooms with closed doors, Olympic wrestlers jump rope inside,
wearing full sweatsuits, hoods worn, hours at this, and he yanks up,
covering the focus, where locker rooms erupt in undress, weigh in
after practice and repetitive exercise, team members fully naked,
waiting to step on the scale before showering. His sides of thick,
stripped twins in diver's position, first time trying yoga, they tip
over, one in each hole of his shorts, full, stretching, weather
changing; and some want to reach in, dig fingers between
any tight warm spots, then pull out and sniff, drop weights
when thinking about it, the world between those thighs.
And he took a look around, shoplifter's last glance
prior to the move, pockets no longer empty, skin
for his eyes only, doing bar pulldowns not stopping
him from watching, amateur bodybuilders go gay
for pay, figure out the taste of best friends, how this
can feel good when it's not far from wrestling,
hands searching, the oblivious beneath stretched
materials, outlined in public, pinned on the mat,
every muscle tense for about three seconds.

LIVING IN THE ICE AGE

Scream, "It's going to snow motherfucker!"
The meteorologists whirling dervishes,
spinning like Wynona Ryder near the end
of *Edward Scissorhands*. Blades flying,
shaved ice eats sky, Depp's block,
lawn iceberg, the size wooly mammoths
are found in, naked humans from 10,000 B.C.
The struggle is real. What day is it?
Meteorologists drunk in a park,
walking runway, blizzard afterbirth,
confetti inside balloons pin popped,
Times Square on New Year's Eve
when the ball drops, wasted paper.
Empty forties in a bush, icicles thick
on rhododendrons, Old English slammed
on weekends, the most famous breaks
into the Macarena, the musical of
Quest for Fire. Everyone scream,
"We're all going to die!" Dinosaur heads
PEZ open, jaw jawing at the sun before
it's gone. Tidal waves freeze mid-splash.
We end up hood ornaments, solid,
stored nuts underground, lucky ones
famous like the next millennium, bones
posed in action, look so good on display.

THEN I SAW ANOTHER BEAST COMING UP OUT OF THE EARTH

We can't say, "It's all for you Damian," son of Satan,
pipsqueak pretending to pole dance in a subway car,
stranger's six-year-old screaming while circling;
one day he'll perform magic, bury us in a tunnel,
sand, selfies, make us remember his name,
stomped on tin of sardines, end of the line
with exploding young men, his girlfriend,
mad, bad, and dangerous to know,
natural born killers minus the trauma.
A nanny hanged herself from the roof.
Like weee, here's the yo-yo, look at me,
busting through a window, tossed car
in a tornado, what causes a maid inside
to scream, turn away. Children on the lawn
watch dead sway. We've got your prom photos,
the suit you wore, sold on eBay 'cause mama
needs the money. We trash origins, homegrown
terrorism, lightning rods struck clean from a roof
and soar drone missile strike. People take cover,
a priest banging church doors, wind picks up.
The beast's aim outstanding, lancing the man
of the cloth in what looks like a park,
top to bottom, shish kebab.
"It's all for you." Guns drawn.
A British photographer follows us,

dishes on the kid's real mother, the jackal
buried in a cemetery guarded by wild dogs.
We can't lose our heads over this, a child
death drops on the subway platform,
a train vanishes in the tunnel, inferno,
drone attacks in a desert,
firecrackers in a tin can,
you'll never see it coming.

CRUISIN' FOR A BRUISIN'

Never got all George Michael in a public bathroom,
the guy next door too close, praying mantis untouchable,
ambush predator eyeing out in the open, actions showing
a urinal who's boss, the wait to ruin it all, allow King Midas
minutes to liquefy, hose white walls with turn everything
to gold, someone ate asparagus, lousy riches,
the presence tap, tap, tapping,
pulling on what changes colors
out the corner of the eye,
waiting because too pee shy,
stuck-in-plumbing panic attack,
self-inflicted beatings, balled fists
pulverizing forehead, closed eyelids,
hundred lashes for the lack of sin,
failed big-time pig bottom,
drown face-first in the nearest toilet,
clean water preferable, gulp air between flushes,
like this is how to get rid of hiccups. Come now officer,
the handcuffs are needed, leather chaps prance
heavy, breathing, aching for hairy thighs,
to be alive, reanimated and ass out,
pop a boner, bull bang public,
praying-mantis arms hook tight, bruise
shoulders, male horns gore insides swollen,
a chance to be arrested before piss makes
an appearance, claw for gold foil, the kind

condoms come in, Midas's favorite, his PrEP pills
turned, royal flush, the age of exploration, bend over
buddy, open and bleeding, a first for everyone, like please
not the handcuffs, photos on the cover of a magazine,
an asshole spitting evidence, decorates tiles
in sugarless gobs, chewed gum.
"What's your definition of dirty baby."
This bathroom is difficult to breathe in.

GO, INDIE, GO

Without antidepressants, the last butter knife
in a utensils drawer during an earthquake.
What if we begged your pardon,
uncrossed our legs on the subway?
Think back on each footstep in public,
segments of sidewalk rock on rapids questioned,
Indiana Jones keeping his eyes open in a cavern,
tiptoes to another ancient prize before triggering
ground to open, the release of killer bees, swarm
masked and shape shifting, locusts approach
blackout, our only crops encased in lungs,
underpants, Indiana dropped his EpiPen
down a drain prior to mountains,
the climb upward. And it's no time
for Jenga or applying nail polish,
not right for carrying a bowl of soup,
gold disaster like a bathtub slipped in.
We are hive heavy, head trauma swelling,
unrecognizable in mirrors. This land, our land;
a field of lightning rods that exists for art's sake.
A psychiatrist advises it's best to continue—
why mess with what's working, no end
to medication, our wood block to bite on,
when loose butter knife is jammed
in a toaster slot, plugged into
a kitchen wall, our popped tiles,
our little fires, no earthquake
can conquer us now.

MISTY WATERCOLOR MEMORIES OF THE WAY WE WERE

So much changed at the Crossroads of the World, rewalk
Forty-seventh Street, that thirteen-floor apartment building
now named, the Somerset, and received a modern awning,
a metal sculpture by an abstract expressionist, junked
outside an uptown museum, dragged sparking over
sidewalk, a tangle of ribcages dug up from local
cemeteries, anyone who previously resided in
that area, can inhale phantoms, the heat of
a tourist's meal, the friction of arms brushing,
covered feet inside thick socks, rubbed steps
on low carpet, the electricity living between each
touch, the near misses, purple blue plasma center pole
released from an Eye of the Storm, specter silent, unseen,
down another crowded city street. We crackle witch on a stick,
say hello to each person in on it, hollered guilty, sniffing the air,
familiar with burnt flesh, every promise made in the past,
the suck of a decade ago—this place not lived in again.

THIS GUEST ROOM MUST BE HAUNTED

Forced to watch a ceiling fan,
its highest setting, attack of pinwheel,
most giant UFO drilled through rooftop,
flickering circle, wash cycle, brain fed Adderall,
this full-size bed in a guest room, where a parent died
two years ago, the mother incapable of waking
the father. He always watched the television
when lights out and good night.
Don't change the channel. One eye
must be open. How can this be comfortable?
Central air on top of it all. The sheer navy valance
shakes atop closed blinds; each panel some undone skirt
a ballet dancer wore during a recital, a female ice skater
twirled in—the bunching on the rod, just picture a waist.
This room not so important, temporary.
The closet where his clothes were kept.
His wife claimed the walk-in
of the master bedroom.
Three toolboxes on the floor under
pants, shirts, jackets, their wire hangers—
a few pieces never worn after being drycleaned,
numbered tags stapled to washing instructions,
narrow ones through buttonholes, sights behind
clear plastic bags, so goddamn long, kinds
that dragged on floors, aging out
of outfits, necessary organs

not functioning, his hours on dialysis,
the air angry, batted out-of-hand particles,
weaved blankets flipped-out ghosties taking
cover when a helicopter lands,
unidentified flying object
destroys worlds.
The fake lilies
on the dresser
need to go.

I'VE HAD THE TIME OF MY LIFE

Like bones matter or the distance from one attraction
to another at a big-city zoo, grandchildren cheer—
the brain says no and no, each word unavailable,
a short man in a raincoat wearing someone
else's glasses, a prescription ten times stronger
to correct another person's vision, trying to do
a crossword puzzle one-handed, standing, crap pen
and a copy of the *Times*. Just answer the question:
birthday, daughter's name, the car model
your husband drives. Late night shower
and a need for help, instead you scream
a gym locker combination, then the phone
number from the first home you lived in.
These three strokes, polar bears now snowmen,
the hippos armored tanks. You spread on the loveseat,
blanket beneath the chin, no plans with the living, the kitchen
floor calling when balance went to sit where someone pulled
the chair out, gag gone wrong, broken arm. A male stilt walker,
says, "Gonna use the crapper"—a giraffe on hind legs clicking
across linoleum, that man married to that woman,
the couple that sleeps in the other bedroom—
some days they are your parents, others strangers.
And who doesn't love company, unlike a coworker
who retired in her seventies and found it impossible
to climb every staircase. Her lipstick crooked then on
her front teeth, her always a cigarette, and strong drinks

in private. Three years later, they found her dead
in her apartment; let's raise a glass in her honor,
to third strokes and Alzheimer's, giving up
when there's nothing to leave home for:
a safari inside a magic show,
a dark cabinet without a trapdoor.

JUST SAY NO

Eye contact resembles death scene,
you reaching get-me-out-of-this-empty-pool
or I can't look down and the scaffolding is loose,
rotted attic floorboards, what carpenter ants ruined,
tooth plaque, flesh-eating bacteria, front-page photo
right before the train pulled in, a man facing a camera,
not even trying to return to the platform, leap
last second from tracks. It's fantasy eyes,
painted nipples on a cold day, the moment
family decides to remove the feeding tube,
the realization that not every kernel will pop, some
burn, fuse black to the inside of a microwaveable bag,
your first days in the big city, your catching your breath,
arms up, at the end of a half marathon a friend talked you
into doing, the goddamn give that runner a cup of cold water,
and first response limps toward home base, says face the ground,
look up, it's not love at first site, it's not follow me home and fulfill
sex-with-a-stranger fantasy number two. No hair braiding.
No undressing in public. Happy endings equal
immediate disqualification.

USEFUL MAN

Beefcake Bob, adult man, once chunky kid serving
checkered overalls, cherry cheeks, like cave person
cosmetics—lift rock, crush, the color red transfers
outdoors on fingers. His baggy camel legs stop
at construction boots, the identical folds
one against the other, oh tired hooves.
Notice the welder mask face out
from his backpack worn over
the chest, his *Star Wars* droid
still riding pouch comfy, wrenches
for ankles, pig-knuckle-sized nuts, bolts,
squeak among thermos, extra T-shirt. Never
mind shoulders, arms, a more slender physique
on *Fantastic Four*'s Thing, linebacker meets chisel
and hammer, a collection of orange chips, fish
tank pebbles, the end of a workday, slowed
down manpower. Sexy but serious,
quiet queen's fetish, too close to
the blowtorch, she's squeezing
thighs, berries, juicing admiration:
the dad in his garage changing oil
in mom's car, preparing for new brake
pads tomorrow morning, weekends outside
Manhattan, barbecue at Bob's, big boy wears
a wife beater, he don't need no fuckin' apron,

says, "It's clobberin' time," kisses a flexed bicep, then flips a well-done burger. Pearl clutches on an N train, she came a little just watching.

FLOODING BASEMENTS AT SIX FLAGS GUANTANAMO PARK

Oscillating clown head in a carnival stand, fill the mouth, poor job
at waterboarding, blow synapses' energy made real in the shape of
an expanding balloon, pink and stretching, a baby eggplant, slight
jiggle visible, thick dog tail unsure, stay down but move a little,
Euro boy cock, like he's twenty or something, commando or
boxers beneath black basketball shorts. Park walkway, benches
homes of barkers, feed dollars, coins obsolete, play big for lack of
need, only want, want, want. Wet face in summer, not drool but sweat,
every doll on the two-wins shelf capable with ball-jointed limbs, necks;
find the figure cloaked in active wear, look past each damn visitor
'cause they're overdressed, tight jeans or khaki midthigh zip up,
okay for bubble butt, too much fabric in the front. The passengers
are restless, fidgeting in seats too small, legs held captive by lap bars.
An urge to jump from the top half of a Ferris wheel, the high point of
the roller coaster's first hill, mouth first, ass first, even hands
extended, some kind of dive, the pull of hidden treasure,
the goddamn it he can't get close enough, sandbar reachable
at low tide for swimmers drift choked, weak, all boardwalk
down the shore, every day a carnival in summer,
imagine what happens when he wears those
in water. Beach weather, pants lowered, promises of
a nude section for sunbathing, clowns wash off makeup
each incoming wave, waterboarded in hot rooms
underground, one window too high up to look out.

Can't see what I want, can't see what I want.
Keep swallowing like a thirsty motherfucker.

THELMA AND LOUIS (SPOILER ALERT: WE DON'T DRIVE OFF A CLIFF)

Pull you off her, start this isn't gather the spring flowers
in this darling's underpants, the stink of your junk
all just five miles on a treadmill, then paced indoors
carrying dumbbells, a football team asleep
in a wet burlap sack, naked pileup, your forearms,
quick to rip garments, say this is how I drive dates home,
porch lights, car interior, the ceiling a circus tent drooping,
every hurricane in the south, flooding our rooftops,
bloated rodent corpses in drain pipes,
everyone's hands get dirty. We corner you,
pretend again, you the victim, today's theme
thrill kill, wrap this shred of baby blanket like a blindfold,
then listen to a man's voice, why we call the hot tub
egg drop soup, offers to dunk you headfirst, a wrist
held hard against your lips, the word *fag*
sliced elbow to palm; he says, "Lick it," like time
to turn you, feed from the master, now it's a headband,
see who's giving you the best blowjob, notice
we're recording this for a gay-for-pay porn site.
Arms shake with lace ruffle sleeves,
we've been here for centuries, the ringmaster
using a megaphone, isn't this how we talk, spittle
on your forehead, the last lisp a just used condom
slapped empty like holy shit it's biting me, a parakeet

snapped into its cage, it shit on your shoulder,
she wasn't asking for it, you've never met him before,
your upper legs, nude wrestlers piss drunk at a titty bar,
lubed then squeezed in one end of an hourglass.
You'll fuck anything with the lights out. Turn over.
We're dropping knees first from a backseat,
T-shirt rolled up, someone dragged
across a driveway, kicked in the stomach.
We've got a spray bottle of weed killer and a knife
here with your name on it. Didn't we tell you
we're not playing games anymore?

BOUNTY

One square of paper towel, the brawniest, stretched beneath
a faucet, it's drip in the kitchen, some secret wiped hard
like this is how you go commando, discuss in public how clean
your bum is, that on occasion you don't wash your hands
before leaving the bathroom. Water spreads who's going to
scrub the counter clean with this sopping wet thing, balance
a short drinking glass in the center, his or her temperament
Monday morning, eyes on the everyday dirty in this steel sink,
and presto it's two-fisted Whack-a-Mole, the shakedown,
a box marked *fragile*, flat sheets of rock candy, clear panes
in a board-game pop bubble, a buzzer sounding like there goes
the last pinch of sand in the hourglass, pencils down, and red
is silly string, we got you broken fuckers in pieces, you dishes,
you mugs, the pint glasses unwrapped last Christmas.
It's a smartphone ringing, the drowned in sagged floors
of the submarine setting, a hey, look at that, hands shaking.
This don't even move, perhaps imagine how cool it could be
if you were the Fantastic Four's Invisible Woman, try out
force fields, a dashed circle your full-body halo;
in 3-D it's a snow globe, you're on water inside
an inflated plastic ball, filmed for a competitive
reality show, like get to the shore first and soak
your fingers in it, some liquid dish soap popular
in the '80s. And there's a window in the bedroom,
a locked door behind you to the apartment.
What time is breakfast? Where are the paper

plates and napkins, potato sacks, a giant slide
to the home below? Do you want to see
which bandage is more absorbent, wear
a diaper like a neck brace, find answers
on the television? Choose a shard
of glass; let's get all *Prom Night*
up in here, collapse on rolls
of paper towels, and watch
everything turn red.

BORN IN THE U.S.A.

Money, money, money, damn chant singsong on Lexington
and 59th, a man with a cane limps past speaking loud,
arm extended, hand carrying an open baseball cap,
mesh liner loaded with change, dollar bills.
He hums what sounds like "Gimme Shelter";
he's gonna fade away. And H&M didn't have
men's corduroy pants despite the appropriate season—
stress of trying on clothing that should fit but sweaty
never squeezes past hips; this male figure
now adult Kewpie doll, god damn fitness,
the U.S. economy, the ability *to accept*
the things I cannot change and the courage
to change the things I can. Perhaps it's time
for new experiences: signing up for tap class,
learning to use a sewing machine, sketching
nude models in studios with charcoals. It's been
since high school the visual meant right this second;
this attention to details cost an extra day of income,
eight additional hours of trying to stay awake.
Perhaps it's important to pick up a trade,
because buildings multiply reversed clips
of a Jenga stack tipped over on tables, good-bye
abandoned residence, kind with planks nailed over
broken windows, very keep zombies out,
the serial killer hoping to clear house,
like every day is Halloween and one day

the power will shut off, the entire eastern
seaboard dark, and carpentry now useful,
as well as weapons and survival skills
in this country called a superpower,
an empire still dominant,
we'll never be refugees,
unbathed, starving,
or half-dead
asylum seekers,
fifty on a lifeboat.

PART TWO

Buried a wristwatch and sat in the dark,
scaled multiple two-floor ranches for comfort
in this body, this person, the ability to exit
the front door, forget sometimes this presence
is a moving target, a seven-year-old boy
walking on his toes, afraid of high shrubbery,
threats on two legs tucked rabid between
garbage, lawn, mouthfuls of spit, chompers,
taller boys foaming over forked tongues, out to bite
thick little thighs, cripple and infect, hypodermics
held stab forward by strangers on the dance floor
of a nightclub, like someone injecting people
with bad blood in the '90s, the fear of HIV when
it was Michael Myers in your bedroom, kitchen knife
already pickaxe flying, an angry miner digging for air.
And time lost running, the can't see lightning flash off
heels, the can't pretend to be a comic book hero,
the ones so in shape dressed in colors, curves,
bags of pills that made you feel funny, the seesaw
in puddles, touching your best friend's genitals
then waking up in wet underwear. The realization
that everyone else already knows; they're waiting
around the corner, holding plastic bags open,
dying to suffocate a faggot, bury you
in panic, unable to tell time facedown.
Years later a push-up to rising on one knee,

slow walk into rooms of men who love men,
and cigarettes and sure you're not gay
and holy crap these people are happy
and why can't I stop walking and why
can't I stop walking, Cher can't even
turn back time, we dance and drug
and kiss and hug, there is naked,
there is yelling, there are two flat feet
in high heels, I walk better in these than
in sneakers. Please talk more than twenty
years later, please forget that *Will & Grace*
once meant something. No need for heads up,
a man laughed out loud down the block, the skip
to the bodega, the French kiss in the park,
it's still snake pit drown me inside a plastic bag,
a stranger's crosshairs on you, my family in
a slasher film. We fight now to make it
to the sequel, in-shape gangs of final girls
lighting candles and strutting through alleys.

LETTING THE DAYS GO BY

Someone says, "This is where it's at,"
like another glacier melted somewhere
Arctic, slain snowmen fallen in battle,
a new cold river drags bodies downhill.
And who has something important to
share, as in raise your arm and wait
for a microphone, it will soar direct shot
into an open hand, death's scythe cuts
air, an audience breathless, blue noses,
darkening fingertips. Everyone claps
and everyone stomps, a Republican
debate, where candidates compare
penis size, and two Democrats believe
Michigan's governor should step down;
this is dated now, irrelevant as of 2017.
And who said, "I'm down with that"?
Another grassland territory, wildlife
sanctuary borderline desert, rhino
skulls and the smallest pebbles. White
Americans and Western Europeans
follow tour guides into brush, carrying
semiautomatic hunting rifles; they paid
out the nose for this, every endangered
story ends beneath boots, kills posted
on social media. College students start
petitions online, face cop cars' sirens,

broken noses, bones in fingers, like news
reports of asteroids moon size and firing
on our course for at least half, and
someone said, "Where's that at?"
A whole side of a volcano
slides from an island into
the ocean; a megatsunami
is heading for the entire
U.S. eastern seaboard,
most likely worse than
mutual assured destruction,
bodies jigsaw puzzles in boxes
fallen from an overhead shelf of
a walk-in closet, disaster on a hardwood
floor, pieces everywhere, some now missing.
Someone sings, "My God! What have I done?!"
and you're pinned by a boulder deep in
a flood zone, watching it all turn blue,
a plastic bag filling with water,
seconds before night explodes,
and land animals join sea life,
float or sink, together, quiet.
"Same as it ever was . . ."
"Same as it ever was . . ."

THE END

ABOUT THE AUTHOR

Robert Siek is the author of the poetry collection *Purpose and Devil Piss* (Sibling Rivalry Press, 2013) and the chapbook *Clubbed Kid* (New School University, 2002). His work has appeared in various publications, such as *Bay Windows, Columbia Poetry Review, Court Green, Painted Bride Quarterly,* the *Good Men Project,* and other places through the years. He lives in Brooklyn and works at a large publishing house in Manhattan.

ABOUT THE PRESS

Sibling Rivalry Press is an independent press based in Little Rock, Arkansas. It is a sponsored project of Fractured Atlas, a nonprofit arts service organization. Contributions to support the operations of Sibling Rivalry Press are tax-deductible to the extent permitted by law, and your donations will directly assist in the publication of work that disturbs and enraptures. To contribute to the publication of more books like this one, please visit our website and click *donate*.

Sibling Rivalry Press gratefully acknowledges the following donors, without whom this book would not be possible:

Liz Ahl	Bill La Civita
Stephanie Anderson	Mollie Lacy
Priscilla Atkins	Anthony Lioi
John Bateman	Catherine Lundoff
Sally Bellerose & Cynthia Suopis	Adrian M.
Jen Benka	Ed Madden
Dustin Brookshire	Open Mouth Reading Series
Sarah Browning	Red Hen Press
Russell Bunge	Steven Reigns
Michelle Castleberry	Paul Romero
Don Cellini	Erik Schuckers
Philip F. Clark	Alana Smoot
Risa Denenberg	Stillhouse Press
Alex Gildzen	KMA Sullivan
J. Andrew Goodman	Billie Swift
Sara Gregory	Tony Taylor
Karen Hayes	Hugh Tipping
Wayne B. Johnson & Marcos L. Martínez	Eric Tran
Jessica Manack	Ursus Americanus Press
Alicia Mountain	Julie Marie Wade
Rob Jacques	Ray Warman & Dan Kiser
Nahal Suzanne Jamir	Anonymous (14)

www.ingramcontent.com/pod-product-compliance
Lightning Source LLC
Chambersburg PA
CBHW062116080426
42734CB00012B/2888